cooking the Lebanese way

Before a Lebanese dinner, a large selection of appetizers, or *mezze*, is served. This *mezze* features kabobs *(back)*, *kibbeh* balls in yogurt *(left)*, eggplant dip *(center front)*, and eggs and beans *(right front)*. (Recipes on pages 34, 35, 36, and 38.)

cooking the
Lebanese way

SUAD AMARI

PHOTOGRAPHS BY ROBERT L. & DIANE WOLFE

easy menu
ethnic
cookbooks

Lerner Publications Company ▪ Minneapolis

Drawings and Map by Jeanette Swofford

Photograph on page 8 courtesy of the National Council of Tourism, Beirut, Lebanon. Photograph on page 11 courtesy of Elsa Marston.

The page border for this book is based on the cedar tree, which also appears on the Lebanese flag. Lebanon is known as "Land of the Cedars" because of the cedar forests that once covered the entire country.

To Etedal and Akram and the rest of the Al-Ashhab family

Library of Congress Cataloging-in-Publication Data

Amari, Suad.
  Cooking the Lebanese way.

  (Easy menu ethnic cookbooks)
  Includes index.
  Summary: An introduction to the cooking of Lebanon featuring such traditional recipes as kabobs, hummus and tahini dip, chard and yogurt soup, and cracked wheat pilaf. Also includes information on the history, geography, customs, and people of this Middle Eastern country.
    1. Cookery, Lebanese—Juvenile literature.
2. Lebanon—Social life and customs—Juvenile literature.
[1. Cookery, Lebanese. 2. Lebanon—Social life and customs] I. Wolfe, Robert L. II. Wolfe, Diane. III. Swofford, Jeanette, ill. IV. Title. V. Series.
TX725.L4A43 1986   641.595692   85-18172
ISBN 0-8225-0913-X (lib. bdg.)

Manufactured in the United States of America

1 2 3 4 5 6 7 8 9 10 94 93 92 91 90 89 88 87 86

Arab pizza is a Middle Eastern version of this popular dish, which probably originated in the Arab world. (Recipe on page 37.)

CONTENTS

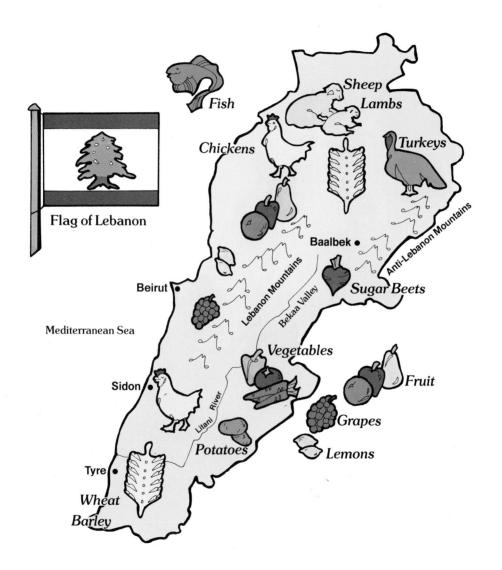

Flag of Lebanon

Fish

Sheep
Lambs

Chickens

Turkeys

Anti-Lebanon Mountains

Baalbek

Lebanon Mountains

Beirut

Bekaa Valley

Sugar Beets

Mediterranean Sea

Vegetables

Fruit

Sidon

Litani River

Grapes

Potatoes

Lemons

Tyre

Wheat
Barley

INTRODUCTION

Although such "foreign" foods as pizza, egg rolls, and tacos now appear on menus in the United States almost as often as hamburgers and french fries, *kibbeh*, *hummus,* and other foods of the Middle East are not as familiar. In recent years, however, Middle Eastern food has become more popular in the United States, largely because of the many restaurants opened by immigrants from that troubled part of the world. Americans have discovered that the Middle Eastern diet, with its emphasis on using fresh fruits and vegetables in a variety of ways, is not only tasty but also healthier and better adapted to modern lifestyles than many heavier European dishes. Lebanon is a country in the very heart of the Middle East, and Lebanese food represents all that is best in the cooking of this historic region.

THE LAND

Lebanon, the smallest country in the Middle East, is only about 30 miles (48 kilometers) wide and 135 miles (216 kilometers) long.

It is bounded on the west by the Mediterranean Sea. On the north, east, and south, the tiny country is hemmed in by larger neighbors —Syria, Jordan, and Israel.

The geography of Lebanon is rugged, with two parallel mountain ranges, the Lebanon and the Anti-Lebanon, running the length of the country. A fertile valley lies between the mountains, and a narrow plain where most of Lebanon's cities are located runs along the Mediterranean coast. Although the amount of land available for raising crops is limited, the country is able to produce almost all its own food. And thanks to the abundant winter rainfall, there is plenty of water.

Like most Mediterranean countries, Lebanon has a generally warm climate. Because summers in the capital city of Beirut can get quite hot, some people escape the heat by visiting the snow-covered mountains nearby. Lebanon is the only country in the Middle East where skiing is a major sport, and one can easily ski in the mountains and swim in the warm waters of the Mediterranean on the same day!

Majestic snow-covered mountains rise behind the Temple of Jupiter at Baalbek, Lebanon.

THE HISTORY

Because of its position at the crossroads of the Middle East, Lebanon has had a very long and complex history. For centuries, Lebanon was ruled by foreign powers, and it has only recently become an independent country.

In ancient times, the stretch of land along the Mediterranean Sea that would one day become Lebanon was part of Phoenicia. Phoenicia was conquered by Alexander the Great in 332 B.C. Nearly 300 years later, the region came under the control of the Roman Empire. During the long years of Roman rule, many people of the area became Christians. In the A.D. 600s, a new religious force, Islam, swept through the Middle East. The followers of Islam, called Muslims, took control of the Eastern Mediterranean, including Palestine, the territory known to Christians as the Holy Land.

During the 1100s and 1200s, armies of Christian soldiers from Europe invaded the Middle East, seeking to take the Holy Land away from the Muslims. The Muslim forces eventually won out. Even though many of its inhabitants remained Christian, Lebanon became absorbed into the Muslim world. From 1516 to 1918, the country was ruled by the Ottoman Turks as a part of the province of Syria. After the Ottoman Empire was defeated in World War I, Lebanon was placed under French control until 1946, when the country finally won its independence.

Unfortunately, independence did not bring lasting peace and prosperity to Lebanon. In recent years, the country has been plagued by terrible internal wars, with groups of Lebanese fighting each other in the streets of Beirut. Lebanon has also been a battleground for other warring countries of the Middle East.

Some of this strife is due to tiny Lebanon's location in the midst of a very unsettled part of the world. Other problems are caused by the religious differences in the country itself. Lebanon is the only Arab country with a large Christian population. Almost half of its citizens are members of the Maronite Church, a division of the Roman Catholic Church. Most of the rest are Muslims belonging to three different sects—Suni, Shiite, and Druse.

Disagreements among these religious groups have been a source of serious conflict.

Despite the conflict and the devastation of war, the Lebanese cling to their old way of life. When I return to visit my family, I still find a wide assortment of fruits and vegetables in the markets of Beirut. Although some of my favorite restaurants are closed (their owners have gone to open establishments in safer places like the United States), my uncles and aunts know of newly opened cafes where we can still sample a wide range of *mezze* dishes, the appetizers for which Lebanese cooking is famous. Even in wartime, life goes on, and the *joie de vivre* (joy of life) of the Lebanese people still survives.

AT THE *SOUK*

Lebanon is considered the most "westernized" country in the Arab world. If you walk down fashionable Hamra Street in Beirut, even in these uncertain times, you will still see expensive shops and sidewalk cafes that resemble those in European cities. Traditional Arab dress and the veil are very rare in Lebanon's large cities. Instead, many Lebanese women wear the latest Paris fashions, and, what is even more surprising in an Arab country, they appear in public in the company of men.

Yet, like the inhabitants of other Arab countries, the Lebanese still prefer to do much of their shopping in street markets, called *souks* in Arabic. A *souk* consists of stalls and shops with their fronts open to the street. When closed, the shops are completely covered by wooden or metal shutters.

In the *souks* of Lebanon, as in all Arab markets, traders in particular kinds of goods are grouped together. There is the street of the spice-sellers and perfume-sellers, the street of the quiltmakers, and so on. In Beirut, there is a huge covered market just for jewelry and precious metals, known as the Gold Market.

The most colorful parts of the *souk*, however, are those that sell foods of all kinds. In the fruit and vegetable section of the market, you will see eggplants, tomatoes, onions, garlic, and fresh herbs such as mint, marjoram, and basil. Various kinds of greens are also available, including spinach, silverbeet, and dark green leaves of *m'loukhia*, a plant unknown outside the Middle East that tastes somewhat like spinach. The spice sellers display huge gunnysacks of brown cumin and coriander seeds, bright red Sudanese pepper (hot ground chili peppers), and golden turmeric and saffron.

Separated from the fruit and vegetable section, the meat market is a busy section of the *souk*. About the only kind of red meat sold at the stalls is sheep—mutton and lamb. There is no beef since the mountainous land of Lebanon is not suitable for grazing cattle. Pork is forbidden to Muslims and is not very popular with the Christian inhabitants of the country. All kinds of poultry as well as rabbits are available in the market, and occasionally there is game such as venison and partridge.

Shopping in the *souk* is an exhausting business, especially in the summer. After finishing our errands, we like to refresh ourselves with cooling drinks sold by street vendors. Lemonade is very popular. The city of Byblos, south of Beirut, is famous for its lemonade, and its main street is lined with

Cherries are one of the many fruits that grow in Lebanon.

stalls selling the beverage. The lemons are, of course, locally grown.

Even on the hottest days of summer, many Lebanese still consider strong, black Arab coffee the most refreshing beverage. We often flavor it with cardamom seed and drink it with either a little sugar, a lot of sugar, or no sugar at all, which makes it very bitter indeed.

Lebanese ice cream is another common summer cooler. My favorite ice cream place is a little stall that sells an enormous variety of fruit flavors, including the delicious mulberry ice cream. For a special treat, you can ask to have your dish of ice cream topped with "merrycream," a mixture of whipped cream and sugar. Here, as everywhere else in Lebanon, the food is fresh and natural.

If you would like to try eating the Lebanese way, the recipes in this book will get you off to a good start. Using them, you will be able to prepare dishes that are simple, appetizing, and truly Lebanese. I am sure you will enjoy this introduction to the delicious cooking of the Middle East.

BEFORE YOU BEGIN

Cooking any dish, plain or fancy, is easier and more fun if you are familiar with its ingredients. Lebanese cooking makes use of some ingredients that you may not know. You should also be familiar with the special terms that will be used in various recipes in this book. Therefore, *before* you start cooking any of the Lebanese recipes in this book, study the following "dictionary" of special ingredients and terms very carefully. Then read through the recipe you want to try from beginning to end.

Now you are ready to shop for ingredients and to organize the cookware you will need. Once you have assembled everything, you can begin to cook. It is also important to read *The Careful Cook* on page 44 before you start. Following these rules will make your cooking experience safe, fun, and easy.

COOKING UTENSILS

colander—A bowl-shaped dish with holes in it that is used for washing or draining food

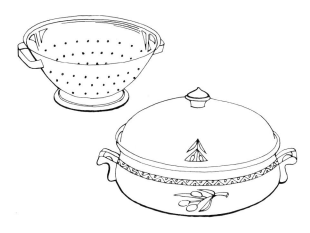

Dutch oven—A heavy pot with a tight-fitting domed lid that is often used for cooking soups or stews

potato masher—A handled utensil with a flat surface for mashing potatoes or other foods

sieve—A bowl-shaped device with very small holes or fine netting used for draining food or forcing small particles from larger pieces of food

skewer—A thin metal rod used to hold small pieces of food for broiling or grilling

slotted spoon—A spoon with small openings in the bowl used to pick solid food out of a liquid

tongs—A utensil shaped either like tweezers or scissors with flat, blunt ends used to grasp food

whisk—A wire utensil used for beating foods by hand

COOKING TERMS

baste—To pour, brush, or spoon liquid over food as it cooks in order to flavor and moisten it

boil—To heat a liquid over high heat until bubbles form and rise rapidly to the surface

broil—To cook food directly under a heat source so that the side facing the heat cooks rapidly

brown—To cook food quickly in fat over high heat so that the surface turns an even brown

garnish—To decorate with a small piece of food such as parsley

knead—To work dough by pressing it with the palms, pushing it outward, and then pressing it over itself

preheat—To allow an oven to warm up to a certain temperature before putting food in it

sauté—To fry quickly over high heat in oil or fat, stirring or turning the food to prevent burning

simmer—To cook over low heat in liquid kept just below its boiling point

Garlic and onions are often sautéed before they are added to other ingredients in a recipe. Here sautéed garlic and onions are lifted out of the pan with a spatula.

SPECIAL INGREDIENTS

allspice—The berry of a West Indian tree, used whole or ground, whose flavor resembles a combination of cinnamon, nutmeg, and cloves

aniseed—The seed of the anise herb, which gives food a strong, aromatic flavor; also called **anise seed**

bulgur—Small cut pieces of dried wheat; also called **cracked wheat**

butter-flavored shortening—Solid vegetable shortening, artificially butter-flavored, available at supermarkets

caraway seed—The seeds of an herb of the parsley family, often used to flavor foods

cardamom seed—A spice of the ginger family, used whole or ground, that has a rich aroma and gives food a sweet, cool taste

cayenne—Ground hot red pepper

chard—A leafy green plant of the beet family

chickpeas—A pale, round legume, available dried or canned

coriander—An herb used ground as a flavoring or fresh as a garnish; also known as *cilantro*

cumin—The seeds of an herb used in cooking to give food a pungent, slightly hot flavor

fennel seed—The seed of an herb of the parsley family used whole or ground in cooking

field bean—A variety of white bean native to the Middle East. Often called *Egyptian field beans,* they are available at Middle Eastern stores, specialty stores, or some supermarkets.

ground ginger—A tangy, aromatic spice made from the underground stem of the ginger plant

ground rice—Rice that has been ground to a fine, flour-like consistency

hummus—A thick paste made of ground chickpeas, spices, and ground sesame seeds

mint—Fresh or dried leaves of various mint plants used in cooking

olive oil—An oil made by pressing olives. It is used in cooking and for dressing salads.

orange flower water—A liquid flavoring made from distilled orange blossoms

pine nuts—The edible seed of certain pine trees

pistachio nuts—Nuts native to Lebanon, now grown in California. The shells and skins are often bright red; the inside of the nut is green.

pita bread—Flat, round loaves of bread common throughout the Middle East. When baked, a puffed pocket of air forms in the center of the bread.

scallions—A variety of green onion

tahini—A paste of ground sesame seeds

white wine vinegar—A vinegar made from white wine. It has a sharp, tangy flavor.

yeast—An ingredient used in baking that causes dough to rise

zaatar—A mixture of wild thyme, sesame seeds, Lebanese sumac seeds, and salt. If unavailable from Middle Eastern groceries, substitute 2 tablespoons thyme, 2 tablespoons sesame seeds, and 1/4 teaspoon salt.

A LEBANESE MENU

Below is a simplified plan for a typical day of Lebanese cooking. The Lebanese names of the dishes are given, along with a guide on how to pronounce them.   *Recipe included in book*

ENGLISH	ARABIC	PRONUNCIATION GUIDE
Breakfast	**Tirwiya**	tir-WEE-ah
Pocket Bread	Pita	PEE-tah
Cheese	Jibneh	JEEB-neh
Olives	Zaytoon	zy-TOON
Arab Coffee	Ahweh	AH-weh
Lunch	**Ghadda**	RHAH-dah
I	I	
*Baked *Kibbeh*	Kibbeh B'zayt	KI-beh b'ZAYT
*Peasant Salad	Fattouche	fah-TOOSH
Olives	Zaytoon	zy-TOON
Fresh Fruit	Khudra Tazeja	HOO-drah tah-ZAY-jah
II	II	
*Chard and Yogurt Soup	Sharabat Silq Bilban	shah-rah-BAHT SILK bil-BAHN
*Fish and Rice Stew	Siyadiyeh	see-yah-DEE-yeh
Fresh Fruit	Khudra Tazeja	HOO-drah tah-ZAY-jah
III	III	
Hummus and *Tahini* Dip	Hummus Bitahine	HOO-moos bit-HEE-neh
*Stuffed Tomatoes	Bandoura Mehshee	bahn-DOO-rah MEH-shee
*Cracked Wheat Pilaf	Burghul Bidfeen	BOOR-gul bid-FEEN
Salad	Salata	sah-LAH-tah
Fresh Fruit	Khudra Tazeja	HOO-drah tah-ZAY-jah

ENGLISH	ARABIC	PRONUNCIATION GUIDE
Snacks	**Helou**	hay-LOO
*Stuffed Pancakes	Atayef Mehshi	ah-TAH-yef MEH-shee
*Festive Milk Pudding	Meghlie	MEG-lee
*Lemonade	Limoonada	lee-moo-NAH-dah
Appetizer	**Mezze**	meh-ZAY
I	I	
*Eggplant Dip	Baba Ganouche	BAH-bah gah-NOOSH
*Arab Pizza	Lahm bil Ajeen	LAHM BIL a-JHEEN
*Eggs and Beans	Foul Mesdames	FOOL mah-DAHM
*Kabobs	Lahm Meshwi	LAHM MESH-wee
II	II	
*_Kibbeh_ Balls in Yogurt	Kibbeh Bilban	KI-beh bil-BAHN
Green Onions	Basal Ahdar	BAH-sahl AH-dahr
Radishes	Fajal	FAH-hahl
Dinner	**Asha**	AH-shah
I	I	
*Garlic Chicken	Djaj Biltoom	d'JAJH bil-TOOM
*Cracked Wheat Salad	Tabbouleh	tah-BOO-leh
Fresh Fruit	Khudra Tazeja	HOO-drah tah-ZAY-jah
Coffee	Ahweh	AH-weh
II	II	
*Cold Meat Loaf	Luffet Bayd	LOO-fet BAYD
Salad	Salata	sah-LAH-tah
Fresh Fruit	Khudra Tazeja	HOO-drah tah-ZAY-jah
Coffee	Ahweh	AH-weh

BREAKFAST/ Tirwiya

As in most of the Middle East, Lebanese breakfasts are quite light. A cup of strong Arab coffee, a piece of pita bread, and cheese and olives are usually enough to keep one satisfied until a midmorning snack or lunch.

LUNCH/ Ghadda

Lebanese lunches are generally light, consisting of soup and salad, perhaps a light main dish, and fresh fruit. A cup of coffee and a sweet snack might help ease hunger pangs during the afternoon.

Ground Lamb Mixture/ Kibbeh

Kibbeh *is one of Lebanon's national foods and is the basis for many dishes.* Kibbeh *is traditionally made from lamb that has been* ground almost to a paste, but it can also be made from regular ground lamb or ground beef. This recipe makes a large amount of kibbeh. *See pages 19 and 34 for ways to use half-recipes of this delicious staple.*

Basic *Kibbeh* Mixture:

2 cups cracked wheat (bulgur)
6 cups water
1 pound ground lamb or beef
1 medium onion, peeled and finely chopped
1 teaspoon cayenne pepper
1 teaspoon salt
½ teaspoon pepper
½ teaspoon cinnamon
¼ teaspoon allspice
¼ teaspoon ginger
½ teaspoon ground coriander
½ teaspoon ground cumin

1. Place cracked wheat in a large bowl. Add 6 cups cold water and set aside for at least 1 hour.
2. Place cracked wheat in a colander and rinse under cold running water. Squeeze

with your hands to remove excess water and set aside.

3. In large bowl, mix meat and onion. Add spices and knead until mixture forms a smooth paste.

4. Put 2 ice cubes in a small glass of water. Knead cracked wheat into meat, adding small amounts of ice water when needed to keep mixture smooth.

5. Cover *kibbeh* and refrigerate about 12 hours or overnight before using.

Makes 2 pounds
(enough for 8 portions)

Baked *Kibbeh*
Kibbeh B'zayt

For this dish, use ½ of the basic kibbeh mixture. You can then use the remaining kibbeh for kibbeh balls in yogurt (see page 34). If you want to serve baked kibbeh for 8 people, use the entire portion of the basic kibbeh mixture, double the amounts of pine nuts and oil, and use two 9- by 13-inch pans.

½ recipe *kibbeh* (see pages 18 and 19)
¼ cup pine nuts
2 tablespoons olive oil

1. Preheat oven to 400°.

2. Thoroughly grease a 9- by 13-inch baking pan.

3. In a medium bowl, stir pine nuts into *kibbeh* mixture, saving a few nuts for decoration. Spread mixture evenly in baking pan.

4. With a knife, make 4 lengthwise cuts, evenly spaced, without cutting all the way through meat. Then make diagonal cuts the same width to make diamond-shaped portions. (Again, do not cut all the way through meat.)

5. Decorate *kibbeh* with pine nuts and drizzle olive oil evenly over mixture.

6. Bake on bottom oven rack for 30 minutes. Then move pan to top rack and bake another 10 minutes.

7. Cut into squares or diamonds and serve hot or cold with salad.

Serves 4

A fresh peasant salad makes an ideal accompaniment to the spicy flavor of baked *kibbeh,* one of Lebanon's national dishes.

Peasant Salad/ Fattouche

Fattouche *is a favorite in Lebanon and is a very good way to use up stale pita bread. You may use any greens in this salad, such as chard, sorrel, or turnip, but they should always be finely shredded.*

2 pieces stale pita bread
1 tablespoon water
1 cucumber, peeled and chopped
1 tomato, chopped
1 green pepper, seeded and chopped
3 scallions, finely chopped
¼ teaspoon pepper
½ cup chopped fresh parsley
¼ cup chopped fresh mint
1 cup finely chopped fresh spinach
**½ head romaine lettuce,
        finely chopped**

Dressing:

1 clove garlic
¼ teaspoon salt

**juice of 2 lemons (about 6
        tablespoons)**
½ cup olive oil

1. Toast or broil pita until crisp and lightly browned. Cut into 1-inch squares and sprinkle with 1 tablespoon water.
2. To make dressing, crush garlic cloves with a garlic press or the back of a spoon. In a small bowl, combine garlic and salt and stir to form a paste. Add lemon juice and olive oil and mix well.
3. In a large bowl, toss remaining ingredients with pita. Sprinkle with dressing, toss again, and serve immediately.

Serves 4 to 6

Hummus and **tahini** dip is a tasty combination of ground chickpeas, ground sesame seed, and spices.

Hummus and *Tahini* Dip/ Hummus Bitahine

Hummus *is a paste made from ground chickpeas, spices, and* tahini—*ground sesame seed. This quick and simple dip is standard fare throughout the Middle East. Canned* hummus *is available in Middle Eastern groceries, specialty stores, or the international or gourmet section of some supermarkets.*

1 cup *hummus*
½ cup *tahini*, thinned according to directions on can
4 hard-cooked eggs
  olive oil
  cayenne pepper
  parsley sprigs for garnish

1. Spread ¼ cup *hummus* on each of 4 small plates. Smooth with a knife.
2. Pour 2 tablespoons *tahini* over each plate of *hummus*.
3. Cut hard-cooked eggs into quarters and arrange at the edges of the plates. Pour a

few drops of olive oil in the center of each plate and sprinkle with a light dusting of cayenne pepper. Garnish with parsley sprigs.

4. Serve with pita bread.

Serves 4

Stuffed tomatoes can be served as an appetizer or teamed with cracked wheat pilaf as part of lunch or dinner. (Recipes on pages 24 and 25.)

Stuffed Tomatoes/ Bandoura Mehshee

Stuffed vegetables are very popular in Lebanon and are served as part of the mezze or as a main course. The filling given here can also be used to stuff zucchini or eggplant.

4 large, ripe tomatoes
1 tablespoon tomato paste
1 tablespoon butter-flavored shortening

Meat filling:

½ pound ground lamb or beef
¼ cup pine nuts
1 teaspoon salt
¼ teaspoon pepper
¼ teaspoon ginger
½ teaspoon cinnamon
¼ teaspoon allspice
¼ teaspoon ground cumin

1. Preheat oven to 350°. Grease a 9- by 9-inch baking dish.

2. Cut tops off tomatoes. Using a spoon, carefully scoop out pulp, making sure not to tear the skin. Save tops and pulp.
3. Place tomatoes in baking dish.
4. In a large skillet, cook meat over medium-high heat until brown, stirring to break into small pieces. Remove meat from skillet with a slotted spoon and place in a medium bowl. Save the grease.
5. Add pine nuts to grease from the meat and sauté over medium-high heat 2 to 3 minutes or until lightly browned.
6. Remove pine nuts from skillet with a slotted spoon and stir into browned meat. Add spices and mix well.
7. Spoon meat mixture into hollowed-out tomatoes. Replace tops on tomatoes.
8. Place pulp from tomatoes in a fine sieve. With the back of a spoon, force pulp through sieve into a medium bowl placed beneath it.
9. In a small saucepan, melt shortening over low heat. Remove from heat and stir in pulp and tomato paste. Pour over tomatoes.
10. Bake for 20 to 30 minutes. Serve hot.

Serves 4

Cracked Wheat Pilaf/ Burghul Bidfeen

Cracked wheat pilaf makes a nutritious and tasty side dish that is served as you might serve rice. In this recipe, the bulgur absorbs the flavors of the ingredients in which it is cooked.

2 cups cracked wheat (bulgur)
½ cup butter-flavored shortening
1¼ cups blanched almonds,
    whole or halved
1 onion, peeled and chopped
2 teaspoons salt
¼ teaspoon pepper
2 10¾-ounce cans (about 3 cups)
    beef or chicken broth

1. Place cracked wheat in a colander and rinse thoroughly. Squeeze with your hands to remove excess moisture. Set aside for at least 1 hour.
2. In a large, heavy saucepan, melt ¼ cup shortening over medium heat. Add almonds and sauté, stirring constantly, about 3 minutes or until lightly browned. Remove with a slotted spoon and drain on paper towels.
3. Add onion and sauté over medium-high heat about 3 minutes. Melt remaining shortening in pan and stir in cracked wheat, salt, and pepper. Cook for 5 minutes, stirring frequently.
4. In another large, heavy saucepan, bring broth to a boil over high heat. Add cracked wheat mixture and almonds. Lower heat and cover pan tightly.
5. Simmer mixture for 40 minutes or until liquid is absorbed and cracked wheat is fluffy and tender. If broth has been absorbed and cracked wheat is not ready, add another ¼ cup boiling-hot broth or water and cook up to 10 more minutes or until broth has been absorbed.
6. Remove pan from heat and let stand, covered, for 15 minutes. Fluff pilaf with a fork and serve hot as a side dish.

Serves 4 to 6

Chard and Yogurt Soup/
Sharabat Silq Bilban

*In the Middle East, yogurt is a staple food
used in many interesting ways. Any
kind of greens, such as turnip, spinach,
or sorrel, may be used instead of chard.*

1 cup cracked wheat (bulgur)
1 pound fresh chard
8 cups water
1 15-ounce can chickpeas
1 teaspoon salt
2½ cups (20 ounces) plain yogurt
    (at room temperature)
1 egg (at room temperature)
2 tablespoons dried mint leaves,
    finely crumbled, or 2 teaspoons
    finely chopped fresh mint for
    garnish

1. Place cracked wheat in a colander and
rinse thoroughly under cold running water.
Let drain until needed.
2. Remove tough stems from chard.
Wash each leaf carefully in cold water
and drain on paper towels.
3. In a large kettle with a lid, bring 3 cups
water to a boil over high heat. Add chard
and return to a boil. Cover and cook
about 3 minutes or until leaves are
thoroughly wilted.
4. Remove chard with a slotted spoon,
place in a bowl, and set aside to cool.
Save the cooking water.
5. Add cracked wheat, chickpeas, and 5
more cups water to chard cooking water
and return to a boil. Lower heat, cover,
and simmer for 1½ hours.
6. While soup is cooking, chop chard
finely with a sharp knife.
7. In a medium bowl, beat together yogurt
and egg. Add chopped chard and about
1 cup of the soup to yogurt mixture.
Stir well in the same direction to prevent
curdling.
8. Remove soup from heat. Gradually add
yogurt mixture, stirring constantly.
Sprinkle each serving with mint and serve
immediately. (Do not reheat or soup
will curdle.)

Serves 4 to 8

Hearty fish and rice stew *(back)* is garnished with crunchy pine nuts. Yogurt, a staple food of the Middle East, makes chard and yogurt soup *(front)* both delicious and nutritious.

Fish and Rice Stew/ Siyadiyeh

Siyadiyeh is a delicious way to prepare fish Lebanese-style. Converted rice is recommended, but regular long-grain rice can be substituted. Any firm, white fish, such as cod, can be used in this recipe.

2 tablespoons vegetable oil
2 tablespoons pine nuts
6 cups water
1 onion, peeled and quartered
2 pounds fish fillets, fresh or
**   frozen (thawed)**
1 cup long-grain converted rice
½ teaspoon cumin
½ teaspoon salt
**   juice of 1 lemon (about 3**
**   tablespoons)**
**   fresh parsley sprigs for garnish**

1. In a small skillet, heat 1 tablespoon oil over medium-high heat. Sauté pine nuts, stirring constantly, about 2 minutes until lightly browned. Drain on paper towels.

2. In a large kettle, bring 6 cups water to a boil over high heat. Carefully add onion and boil 15 to 20 minutes or until soft. Remove onion with a slotted spoon and drain in a colander. Save cooking water.

3. Place onion in a bowl and mash with a potato masher or puree in a blender.

4. Add fish and onion to onion cooking water and bring water back to a boil over high heat. Reduce heat, cover pan, and simmer about 30 minutes or until fish is tender. Remove fish with slotted spoon. Save cooking water.

5. In a large saucepan, heat remaining oil over medium-high heat. Add rice and cumin and cook, stirring constantly, for 3 minutes. Add salt and 2 cups of the fish broth. Cover pan and cook on low heat about 20 minutes or until rice is fluffy and liquid is absorbed.

6. Add lemon juice to remaining fish broth and reheat slowly over medium-low heat.

7. Arrange rice on a serving platter and place fish on rice. Pour reheated broth over fish. Garnish with pine nuts and parsley.

Serves 4

SNACKS/
Helou

Like most Arabs, Lebanese people do not eat a lot of desserts, but sweets are enjoyed as midday snacks or on special occasions. Honeyed pastries and candies are eaten during the day with cups of strong black coffee or mint-flavored tea. Generally, milk-based puddings are the only desserts served after a meal, most often at lunchtime.

Lemonade/
Limoonada

Lemonade is a favorite drink of the Lebanese, both young and old, especially during hot weather. If you use freshly picked lemons, add only half the amount of sugar. If you don't have a blender, grate the lemon peel and squeeze the juice from the lemon. Shake together all ingredients in a large jar, strain, and serve.

2 lemons
2 tablespoons sugar
6 ice cubes
3 cups cold water
2 teaspoons orange flower water (optional)
4 slices lemon for garnish

1. If the lemons are thick skinned, cut off and discard the two end pieces. Cut each lemon into 4 to 6 pieces and place in a blender along with any juice that escaped during cutting.
2. Place lid firmly on blender and blend on maximum speed for 3 to 5 seconds.
3. Add remaining ingredients and blend again on high speed for 30 seconds. Pour through a sieve into a serving pitcher.
4. Serve lemonade in tall glasses with extra ice and lemon slices.

Serves 4

Festive milk pudding and stuffed pancakes are refreshing snacks, especially when served with ice-cold lemonade.

Festive Milk Pudding/ Meghlie

Meghlie *is served to visitors when a child is born. It is very strongly flavored with aniseed, so you may want to use less if you do not like the taste of anise. Use either ground rice cereal for infants or the sweet Japanese rice flour called* mochi, *which can be found in the international section of the supermarket.*

½ **cup ground rice**
3 **to 3½ cups water**
½ **cup sugar**
½ **teaspoon aniseed**
½ **teaspoon caraway seed**
½ **teaspoon fennel seed**
⅛ **teaspoon ground ginger**
2 **tablespoons chopped almonds**
2 **tablespoons chopped**
    pistachio nuts
2 **tablespoons chopped walnuts**

1. In a medium bowl, combine ground rice and ¼ cup cold water. Gradually stir in more water until mixture forms a smooth paste. Add sugar and spices and mix well.
2. In a large saucepan, bring 2½ cups water to a boil over high heat. Add ground rice mixture gradually, stirring constantly to prevent lumps from forming. Continue to stir until mixture boils again.
3. Reduce heat to low. Cover and simmer, stirring occasionally to prevent mixture from sticking to bottom of pan, for about 10 minutes until pudding is thick enough to coat the back of a spoon.
4. Allow pudding to cool slightly before pouring into a glass serving bowl or individual bowls. Cool to room temperature and refrigerate.
5. Sprinkle pudding with chopped nuts and serve cold.

Serves 4

Stuffed Pancakes/
Atayef Mehshi

*These delicious pancakes are sold in the
souk in the winter. They are eaten by
Lebanese Moslems on all festive occasions,
especially after the month-long fast of
Ramadan, which is the equivalent of
Christianity's Lent. Although the flavor
and texture will not be the same, you can
simplify the recipe by using any pancake
batter mix instead of the yeast mixture
given here.*

Filling:

2 cups chopped walnuts
3 tablespoons sugar
2 teaspoons cinnamon

Syrup:

**1 cup pancake syrup or dark corn
      syrup**
**½ tablespoon orange flower water
      (optional)**

Batter:

1 envelope active dry yeast
1 teaspoon sugar
1¼ to 2 cups lukewarm water
1½ cups all-purpose flour
½ cup vegetable oil (for frying)

1. Dissolve yeast and sugar in ½ cup warm
water. Cover lightly with a damp cloth
and leave in a warm place for about 20
minutes or until mixture begins to foam.
2. In a small bowl, mix walnuts, sugar,
and cinnamon. Set aside.
3. In another small bowl, combine syrup
and orange flower water. Set aside.
4. Warm a large mixing bowl by rinsing
with hot water and drying thoroughly.
Sift flour into warmed bowl. Make a
depression in the center, pour in yeast
mixture, and beat into the flour. Continue
beating, gradually adding water until
mixture is the consistency of pancake
batter.
5. Cover mixture with a damp cloth and
leave in a warm place for 1 hour or
until bubbly.

6. Heat a heavy skillet or omelette pan over high heat. When hot, add 1 teaspoon oil and swirl to coat skillet evenly.

7. Pour ¼ cup batter into pan. Tilt pan gently to even out batter, but keep pancake fairly thick and round. Cook until it begins to bubble and comes away easily from pan. Cook only one side of pancake. Repeat with remaining batter, adding oil to pan as needed.

8. Put 2 tablespoons filling on uncooked side of each pancake and fold in half. Pinch edges together firmly to keep filling in place.

9. Pour 2 tablespoons oil into skillet and fry folded pancakes about 2 to 3 minutes on each side or until golden brown. (Add more oil as needed.) Drain well on paper towels.

10. Dip pancakes in syrup mixture while they are still warm and serve with sour cream or cottage cheese.

Serves 4 to 6

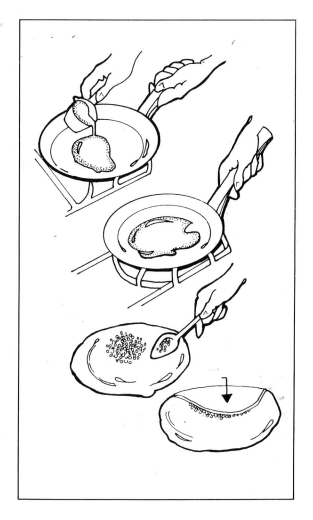

APPETIZERS/ Mezze

Mezze, or appetizers, are a very important part of Lebanese cuisine. Before dinner, a large selection of appetizers in tiny dishes is set out for diners. *Mezze* may include such foods as vegetables, *kibbeh* balls, savory pastries, yogurt, cheese, and olives. Lebanese restaurants compete with each other on the number of *mezze* dishes they offer and may serve as many as 70!

Kibbeh Balls in Yogurt/ Kibbeh Bilban

The flavor of yogurt combines well with meat, as in these delicious meatballs. Keep them small (walnut-sized) so that they cook thoroughly; Middle Easterners like their lamb well done.

½ **recipe basic *kibbeh*
 mixture (see pages 18 and 19)**
2½ **cups (20 ounces) plain yogurt**

1 **tablespoon cornstarch**
1 **teaspoon salt**
3 **cloves garlic, crushed**
2 **tablespoons dried mint,
 finely crumbled**
2 **tablespoons butter or margarine**

1. Roll *kibbeh* mixture into 1-inch balls and set aside.
2. In a large, heavy saucepan, stir together yogurt and cornstarch. Gradually bring to a boil over medium heat, stirring constantly in the same direction to prevent curdling.
3. Reduce heat to simmer. Add salt, crushed garlic, mint, and butter and stir until smooth.
4. Add *kibbeh* balls to yogurt mixture and stir very carefully. Continue to simmer for 20 minutes. Serve as *mezze* or with plain boiled rice for a main course.

Serves 6

Eggplant Dip/
Baba Ganouche

Eggplant dip is a favorite throughout the Middle East, where the eggplant is usually cooked over an open flame, giving the pulp a smoky flavor. Baking it directly on your oven rack will give the eggplant a similar flavor. Baba ganouche *makes a great party dip.*

**1 large eggplant
juice of 2 lemons (about 6
   tablespoons)
4 tablespoons tahini, thinned
   according to directions
   on can
3 cloves garlic
1½ teaspoons salt
4 tablespoons chopped fresh
   parsley for garnish**

1. Preheat oven to 400°.
2. Prick eggplant several times with a fork. Place on oven rack and bake for 30 minutes or until very soft. Remove from oven and cool.
3. When eggplant is cool enough to handle, peel off skin. Cut eggplant into chunks, place in medium bowl, and mash with a potato masher or puree in a food processor until smooth. Beat in lemon juice and *tahini.*
4. In a small bowl, crush garlic into the salt with the back of a spoon. Stir into eggplant mixture.
5. Spread mixture over four small plates as for *hummus* and *tahini* dip (see page 22) or serve in one dish. Garnish with parsley. Eat *baba ganouche* by scooping it up with pieces of pita bread.

Serves 4

Kabobs/
Lahm Meshwi

Meshwi *is the most common meat dish of the Middle East and probably the most delicious as well. Serve a few pieces of the meat and vegetables as* mezze, *or serve a skewerful or two per person with rice and salad as a main course. Use lean sirloin tip or chuck steak for beef kabobs, leg of lamb is best for lamb kabobs. Inexpensive metal skewers are available at most supermarkets.*

½ **cup olive oil**
4 **cloves garlic, crushed**
1 **teaspoon ground cumin**
1 **teaspoon ground coriander**
1 **teaspoon salt**
½ **teaspoon pepper**
2 **pounds beef or lamb, cut**
  into 2-inch cubes
4 **onions, peeled and quartered**
2 **green peppers, seeded and**
  cut into 2-inch squares

1. In a large bowl, combine oil, garlic, and spices and mix well. Add meat and stir until well coated. Refrigerate for at least 2 hours or overnight.
2. One hour before cooking, remove meat from refrigerator. Place 1 cube of meat onto skewer, then add 1 piece of onion and 1 piece of green pepper. Repeat meat/onion/green pepper sequence until 4 skewers are filled and all ingredients used up.
3. Place skewers in a shallow broiling pan. Broil for 10 minutes, then turn skewers over and broil 10 more minutes or until meat has browned. Brush kabobs with oil mixture several times while broiling.
4. Serve hot.

Serves 4

Arab Pizza/
Lahm bil Ajeen

This dish has many variations throughout the Arab world. Although the name varies slightly, it always means the same — "meat in dough." Even the Italian word "pizza" comes from the Arabic word for bread, so pizza probably originated in the Arab world.

**2 packages pizza dough mix
   (enough to make 2 12-inch
   pizzas)**
**1 recipe meat filling (see
   stuffed tomatoes,
   steps 4 through 6, page 24)**
2 tablespoons white wine vinegar
2 tablespoons lemon juice
**¼ cup butter-flavored
   shortening**

1. Preheat oven to 450°.
2. Prepare 1 package pizza dough according to directions on package. Divide dough into 4 pieces. Roll each piece into a ball and flatten. With a rolling pin, roll out each ball into a round about 4 inches in diameter. Repeat with second package of pizza dough. Place rounds on greased cookie sheets.
3. In a medium bowl, mix prepared meat filling with vinegar and lemon juice.
4. Spread filling over rounds of dough, leaving a narrow margin at the edge.
5. In a small saucepan, melt shortening over medium heat. Brush over top of each pizza, coating both the filling and the uncovered edges of the dough.
6. Bake pizzas for 15 minutes or until edges of dough are golden brown. Serve warm.

Makes 8 pizzas

Eggs and Beans/ Foul Mesdames

Traditionally made during Lent, this nourishing, meatless dish is often eaten as a main course, especially in poorer households. More often, however, it is eaten as an appetizer. Middle Eastern grocery stores and the international sections of some supermarkets sell canned Egyptian field beans especially for this dish. If you cannot get them, use canned kidney or pinto beans instead.

**2 15-ounce cans of beans, undrained
2 cloves garlic, peeled and
    finely chopped
2 tablespoons olive oil
    juice of 1 lemon (about 3
    tablespoons)
1 teaspoon salt
¼ teaspoon pepper
4 hard-cooked eggs, quartered
4 tablespoons chopped parsley
    for garnish**

1. In a large saucepan, combine beans and their liquid with garlic, olive oil, and lemon juice. Add salt and pepper and mix well. Simmer over medium heat, stirring occasionally, about 10 to 15 minutes or until heated.
2. Pour beans into individual bowls. Arrange hard-cooked egg pieces on top of each bowl, sprinkle with parsley, and serve.

Serves 4

DINNER/ Asha

After the *mezze*, the main dinner items are served. A meat or fish entree is served with Lebanon's two staples, rice and cracked wheat, in some form. A large salad and a cooked vegetable dish are almost always included as well.

Cracked Wheat Salad/ Tabbouleh

Cracked wheat, called tabbouleh *(often spelled* tabouli*) in Arabic, was probably the very first food known to human civilization. It is also one of the most popular foods in Lebanon, which shows that cracked wheat has definitely withstood the test of time! This refreshing, flavorful salad is very typically Lebanese.*

2 cups cracked wheat (bulgur)
1 onion, peeled and finely chopped
4 large tomatoes, chopped
2 bunches scallions, finely chopped (about 1 cup)
2 small cucumbers, peeled and chopped
½ cup olive oil
juice of 2 lemons (about 6 tablespoons)
1 teaspoon salt
¼ teaspoon pepper
6 tablespoons chopped fresh parsley
3 tablespoons chopped fresh mint or 1 tablespoon dried mint
6 leaves romaine lettuce

1. Place cracked wheat in a colander and rinse under cold running water. Squeeze with your hands to remove excess water and drain for 1 hour.
2. In a large mixing bowl, combine cracked wheat with all remaining ingredients except lettuce.
3. Line a salad bowl with lettuce leaves and add cracked wheat mixture. Chill before serving.

Serves 4 to 6

Two favorite Lebanese dishes are the colorful cracked wheat salad, also called *tabbouleh,* and garlic chicken, served with a zesty garlic sauce.

Garlic Chicken/
Djaj Biltoom

This dish was a specialty of the Marouche Restaurant, located across from the American University in Beirut. Through the years many hungry students have enjoyed this special chicken dish.

**4 cloves garlic, peeled and
    finely chopped
1 teaspoon salt
    juice of 1 lemon (about 3
    tablespoons)
¼ cup olive oil
2 to 2½ pounds chicken pieces**

Sauce:

**1 whole head garlic, cloves
    separated and peeled
1 teaspoon salt
1 cup olive oil
2 tablespoons lemon juice
1 potato, peeled and boiled**

1. In a large bowl, mix first 4 ingredients. Add chicken pieces and stir until coated. Lightly cover bowl with a cloth and let stand 4 hours at room temperature or overnight in refrigerator.
2. Preheat oven to 375°. Place chicken pieces in a roasting pan. Save oil mixture.
3. Roast chicken for 1½ hours, uncovered, basting with oil mixture every 15 minutes.
4. In a medium bowl, prepare sauce. Crush garlic cloves into salt with the back of a spoon. Add 1 tablespoon olive oil to garlic mixture and beat well. When oil is completely absorbed, stir in a few drops lemon juice. Repeat until ¼ cup oil and 1 tablespoon lemon juice have been used up.
5. Put garlic and oil mixture in blender. Add remaining oil, lemon juice, and potato. Blend until mixture looks like shiny whipped cream. (If you don't have a blender, mash the potato, add to remaining ingredients, and beat vigorously with a wire whisk.)
6. Place chicken pieces on a serving platter. Serve hot with small dishes of garlic sauce for dipping.

Serves 4 to 6

Cold meat loaf, a Lebanese version of a familiar dish, has the surprise of hard-cooked eggs baked in the center.

Cold Meat Loaf/
Luffet Bayd

This is a delicious Lebanese version of a traditional North American dish. Eaten cold, it is good with salad and perfect for picnics—a true summer dish.
In Lebanon, this meat loaf is trussed, or tied, with string and cooked in a Dutch oven instead of wrapped in foil. Both methods keep the loaf from falling apart while baking and produce the same delicious results.

1 pound ground beef or lamb
½ teaspoon cinnamon
½ teaspoon zaatar (see page 15)
1 onion, peeled and finely chopped
1 teaspoon salt
½ teaspoon pepper
½ teaspoon ground cumin
3 tablespoons chopped fresh parsley
3 hard-cooked eggs, shells removed

1. Preheat oven to 375°.
2. In a medium bowl, combine meat,

cinnamon, zaatar, onions, salt, pepper, and cumin. Knead thoroughly.

3. Place a strip of aluminum foil, about 14 inches long, on work surface. Place meat mixture on foil.

4. Wet your hands and shape mixture into a 3½- by 8-inch oblong about ½-inch thick. Sprinkle meat with parsley.

5. Arrange hard-cooked eggs end to end in the center of mixture. Shape mixture over eggs to form a loaf.

6. Wrap aluminum foil tightly around meat. Place in roasting pan and bake 40 minutes. (See diagram.)

7. Remove meat loaf from oven. Keeping your face away from the hot steam, carefully unwrap foil using oven mitts and a fork. Pierce loaf with a sharp knife. If juices from center are no longer pink, meat loaf is done. If not, wrap package again and return to oven for 15 minutes.

8. Leave loaf on unwrapped foil to cool. When cool, refrigerate, uncovered, until cold. Slice and serve with salads.

Serves 4 to 6

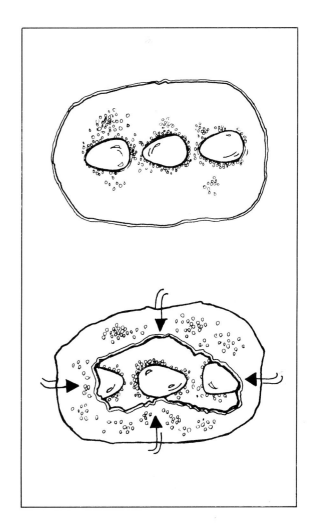

THE CAREFUL COOK

Whenever you cook, there are certain safety rules you must always keep in mind. Even experienced cooks follow these rules when they are in the kitchen.

1. Always wash your hands before handling food.
2. Thoroughly wash all raw vegetables and fruits to remove dirt, chemicals, and insecticides.
3. Use a cutting board when cutting up vegetables and fruits. Don't cut them up in your hand! And be sure to cut in a direction *away* from you and your fingers.
4. Long hair or loose clothing can easily catch fire if brought near the burners of a stove. If you have long hair, tie it back before you start cooking.
5. Turn all pot handles toward the back of the stove so that you will not catch your sleeve or jewelry on them. This is especially important when younger brothers and sisters are around. They could easily knock off a pot and get burned.

6. Always use a pot holder to steady hot pots or to take pans out of the oven. Don't use a wet cloth on a hot pan because the steam it produces could burn you.
7. Lift the lid of a steaming pot with the opening away from you so that you will not get burned.
8. If you get burned, hold the burn under cold running water. Do not put grease or butter on it. Cold water helps to take the heat out, but grease or butter will only keep it in.
9. If grease or cooking oil catches fire, throw baking soda or salt at the bottom of the flame to put it out. (Water will *not* put out a grease fire.) Call for help and try to turn all the stove burners to "off."

METRIC CONVERSION CHART

WHEN YOU KNOW		MULTIPLY BY	TO FIND	
MASS (weight)				
ounces	(oz)	28.0	grams	(g)
pounds	(lb)	0.45	kilograms	(kg)
VOLUME				
teaspoons	(tsp)	5.0	milliliters	(ml)
tablespoons	(Tbsp)	15.0	milliliters	
fluid ounces	(oz)	30.0	milliliters	
cup	(c)	0.24	liters	(l)
pint	(pt)	0.47	liters	
quart	(qt)	0.95	liters	
gallon	(gal)	3.8	liters	
TEMPERATURE				
Fahrenheit (°F) temperature		5/9 (after subtracting 32)	Celsius (°C) temperature	

COMMON MEASURES AND THEIR EQUIVALENTS

3 teaspoons = 1 tablespoon

8 tablespoons = ½ cup

2 cups = 1 pint

2 pints = 1 quart

4 quarts = 1 gallon

16 ounces = 1 pound

INDEX

*(recipes indicated by **bold face** type)*

ABOUT THE AUTHOR

Suad Amari was born in Beirut, Lebanon. She worked in the Lebanese branch of an American bank before coming to the United States with her husband in 1974. Amari tries to keep in contact with her many relatives in Lebanon, including her parents and brothers. She misses the close-knit family life she enjoyed in Lebanon and hopes to return one day with her husband and children when peace is restored. In the meantime, Amari enjoys cooking her native Lebanese cuisine and sharing it with her friends in California.

easy menu *ethnic* cookbooks